Artists of
HANDCRAFTED
FURNITURE
at Work

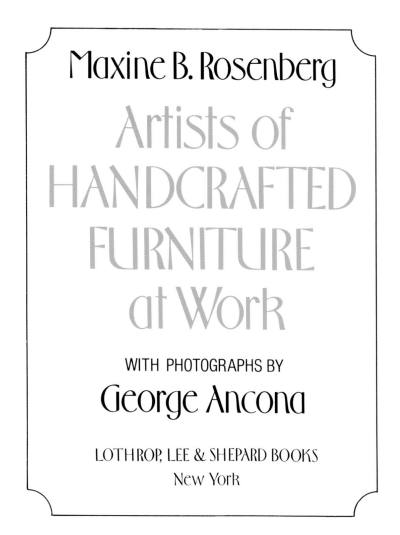

Maxine B. Rosenberg

Artists of HANDCRAFTED FURNITURE at Work

WITH PHOTOGRAPHS BY

George Ancona

LOTHROP, LEE & SHEPARD BOOKS
New York

Printed in the United States of America
Designed by Sylvia Frezzolini
First Edition

1 2 3 4 5 6 7 8 9 10

Library of Congress Cataloging in Publication Data
Rosenberg, Maxine B.   Artists of handcrafted furniture at work.
Summary: Four furniture-makers discuss how they design and make one-of-a-kind chairs, desks, tables, or other furniture that will go into homes, offices, and museums. 1. Furniture making—Juvenile literature. 2. Furniture design—Juvenile literature. [1. Furniture making. 2. Furniture makers. 3. Furniture design. 4. Occupations] I. Ancona, George, ill. II. Title. TT194.R67   1988   749.213   87-29342
ISBN 0-688-06875-8

To Dad—For his spirit and joy of life
MBR

For Jean Seidenberg
GA

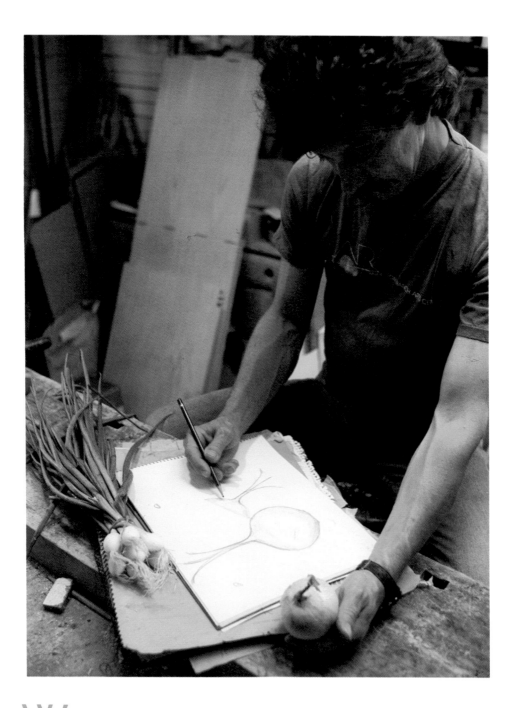

When David Ebner harvested his home-grown onions, something about their shape made him think about building a chest for storing blankets and sweaters.

Three months later, Ebner completed the chest. Made completely of wood, it looks like an overgrown onion.

9

Graham Blackburn, Rosanne Somerson, and Alphonse Mattia also are furniture-makers who look at shapes around them in the everyday world for ideas to put into their work. A portion of a bridge or branches of a tree might prompt thoughts for a new project. A fish skeleton, cartoons on television, and toys in a store have sometimes set ideas into motion.

Creative artists may store ideas in their minds for years and years before using them, or they may go to work on them immediately. Ebner, Blackburn, Somerson, and Mattia, though they work separately, all use their ideas to create chairs, desks, tables, or other furniture that will go into homes, offices, and sometimes museums. Because they handcraft each piece, no two pieces of furniture are exactly alike.

At one time, all furniture was handcrafted. When power-driven machines were invented late in the eighteenth century, it became possible to speed up the production of objects in common use by tooling machines to produce the same item over and over. Because a chair could be made faster if a machine produced its parts, it was cheaper too. Eventually, machines were developed that could do much of the assembly of items as well. Mass-produced items became popular because of their low cost, and most people became accustomed to the sameness of the furnishings of their homes.

The enchantment with dishes, clothing, toys, and furniture that look just like everyone else's began to fade when people noticed they had to be replaced often. Great-grandmother's handcrafted hope chest was as sturdy and useful as the day it was made, but one bought just ten years ago was falling apart. It became apparent that mass-produced items might not be as economical as they seemed.

In the 1960s a new crafts movement began to emerge. Artists responded to people who were willing to pay more for objects that were well made by handcrafting original designs. The movement caught on as people began to appreciate living with objects that were uniquely beautiful and useful as well.

An artist's ideas for design depend on his or her interests. One artist may be inspired by the shapes found in nature, while another may find appealing shapes in mechanical devices, such as cars or trucks.

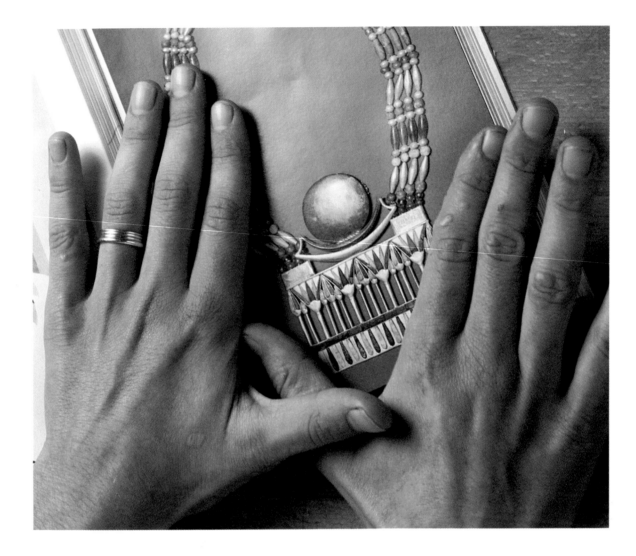

Rosanne Somerson favors geometric forms. Her
background in photography has enabled her to
visually frame small shapes from larger
compositions. A portion of an ancient Egyptian
necklace in a museum caught her eye and prompted
her to make the "High-heeled Coffee Table." The
geometric shapes in primitive African masks and in
a 1920s Art Deco poster gave her ideas for two other
tables.

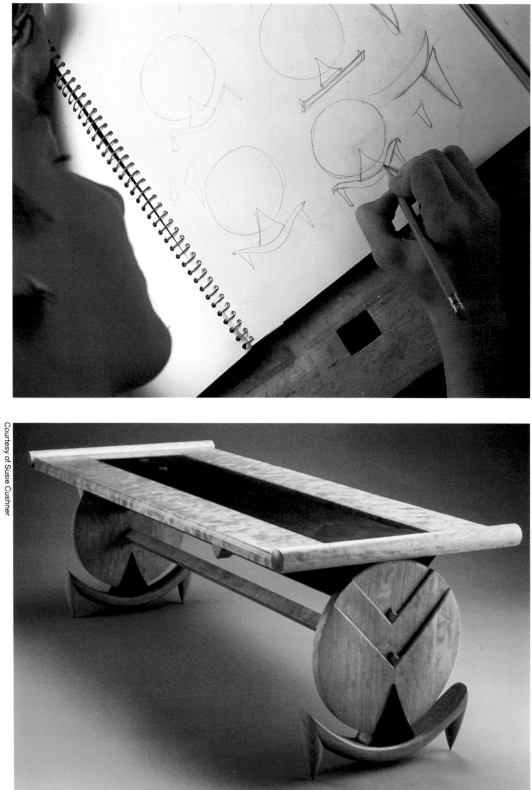

Alphonse Mattia enjoys watching horror movies on television. An old Frankenstein film inspired him to make a valet. Mattia, who has an expressive

sense of humor and likes to joke, added a head to his valet and shaped it like a brain, which he based on the brain mix-up in the movie. He designed his valet to make it useful for both women's and men's clothing.

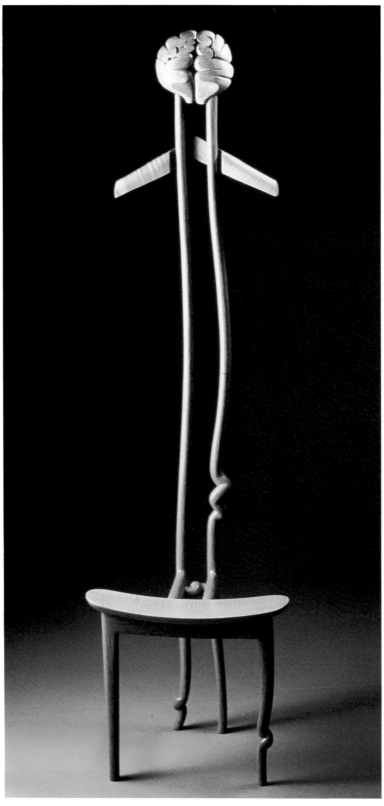

Like most people, creative artists tend to have a wide variety of interests. It isn't unusual for an artist's ideas to come from many different sources. Architectural forms—especially those of Japanese and Chinese origin—particularly appeal to David Ebner, but he also responds to organic shapes, such as those found in plants and animals. One night, while eating duck for dinner, Ebner became intrigued with the bird's breastbone.

"It rocked when I played with it," he says. Ebner used the shape to create a rocking chair, a music stand, a dictionary stand, and a coffee table.

As a child, Ebner shared his father's woodworking hobby. "I had already made my own baseball bat by the time I was nine," he boasts. Ebner's real training came in high school, however, where one teacher in particular taught him the techniques of fine woodworking craftsmanship. When Ebner entered college, his ability to construct well-made furniture placed him far ahead of most other students.

Graham Blackburn's inspiration is antique furniture created by craftsmen two or three hundred years ago. He visits museums and reads books about art and furniture to learn more about the design and proportion of pieces made long ago. When Blackburn fashions a piece with a contemporary look, he draws upon ideas from both the past and the present. He will create a table suited for twentieth-century needs but detail its legs with carvings styled after those used by Hepplewhite, the eighteenth-century English cabinetmaker.

Blackburn has always been interested in history. "I lived in England as a child, and when my school class went on trips to Roman ruins I'd come home with pieces of broken pottery and tiles," he recalls. At age eleven, Blackburn saved enough money to buy antique woodworking tools. Blackburn's love of wood, his involvement with history, talent in art, and the influence of his father—who built houses— account for his decision to pursue furniture-making as a career. By the time Blackburn enrolled in college, he had already begun an apprenticeship to an English cabinetmaker.

Alphonse Mattia learned to handle wood from his father, who was a carpenter. "From the time I was a kid, I made my own toys and model airplanes," Mattia reports. "Then as a teenager I worked in a hobby shop making displays and painting models for exhibits." The owners of the shop, impressed with Mattia's original designs, urged him to go further with his talent. Today Mattia creates whimsical, cartoon-like furniture, as well as classically styled pieces. He also teaches furniture-making at a college, and in his spare time builds model airplanes and helicopters.

Not all furniture-makers are experienced with woodworking when they begin working with wood. Rosanne Somerson was an artist who chose wood as her medium of expression. She could as easily have chosen clay, glass, or paint.

When Rosanne began college, photography, sewing, and sketching interested her most. As a child, Rosanne had watched her father build their house, and she recalls loving the smell and feel of wood. She tried to take a shop course in junior high school, but girls weren't permitted. At college, she realized how attracted she'd always been to the three-dimensional aspects of wood and wood forms and decided to work with it as an art medium.

"Ten thumbs," her college instructor said of her, and expressed doubt that she could ever master woodworking techniques. That summer, Somerson went to Scotland to practice using tools properly. For two months she made wooden whiskey barrels, becoming the first female cooper apprentice in Scottish history. Today, Rosanne Somerson's furniture is sold throughout the United States and is exhibited in museums.

Though individual furniture-makers may have reasons unique to themselves for choosing the craft, they all share certain feelings—a love for wood and the desire to bring fine workmanship and artistic design into daily living. By studying techniques used in the past by master furniture-makers, such as joining drawers with dovetail fittings, twentieth-century craftspersons have learned how to give their work the exacting care that makes their furniture endure. Some handcrafters of furniture guarantee their work for their lifetime.

Emphasis on design is a major difference between modern handcrafters and those of the past. For the old masters, the function of a piece was more important than its form or design. There is even a saying, "Form *always* follows function," that was a motto for anyone who created useful objects. Today, most artists of handcrafted furniture place equal emphasis on function and design.

David Ebner recalls having to make a conscious effort to give his pieces pleasing designs that also functioned well. When he began furniture-making at college, he was more concerned with the technique of making the piece, and how it would suit its purpose when finished, than with how it looked. His teacher advised him to look more closely at shapes around him and to try to use them to add more interest to his work. As an aid to observation, he developed the habit of sketching everyday objects that appealed to him.

Twenty years later, Ebner rarely walks down a street or eats a meal without observing forms. Each time he leaves his house he stuffs his back pocket with four or five drawing pens. When he returns he usually has several sketches made on napkins or scraps of paper, which he pins up on his shop wall. Eventually a shape sketched at an idle moment will turn up in one of his finished pieces.

Pleasing design was a first concern for Rosanne Somerson. "I had to learn the techniques of making my work function well," she says. "Furniture that is used has more life. I want my furniture to be a part of people's lives.

"As people live with handcrafted furniture," Somerson explains, "they discover surprises—details that aren't immediately apparent—that add to their enjoyment. A decorative pattern may be repeated inside a drawer, or some other place not on display—some small detail that says the maker was paying attention even to the places not on view."

David Ebner is also concerned about how his furniture stands up under use. When he designed his modern version of an outdoor Victorian bench, he researched and tested materials to make certain it would endure outside. "Thirty years from now people will sit on this bench and say it is still beautiful," he boasts.

A special feature of Graham Blackburn's work is the secret compartments he puts into his pieces. Blackburn got the idea from furniture-makers of the seventeenth and eighteenth century. "There were no safe deposit boxes in banks then, so people hid their money and private papers in secret drawers built into desks, bureaus, and tables," he explains.

If asked where he's placed a hidden compartment, Blackburn grins and says, "It wouldn't be a secret if I told."

Blackburn, like the cabinetmakers who inspired his secret compartments, places the function of a piece before its design. "I want my furniture to be admired," he says, "but comfort and use must come first."

The design of Alphonse Mattia's furniture is contemporary. He interprets the geometric form of a modern bridge in the shape he gives to an elegant table.

To add fun and variety to furniture, he paints, bleaches, or grains wood to give it the look of Formica or metal. "While traditional furniture-makers use wood only as it exists in nature, I like widening the world of wood by taking a more artistic approach," Mattia explains.

Just as furniture-makers differ in their approach to design, they also vary in how they make preliminary sketches for a piece. Rosanne Somerson fills a whole notebook with detailed drawings of what she has in mind before beginning a piece. Sometimes she will arrange a pattern of cutout shapes of wood and tissue paper, similar to the way she lays out a dress pattern when sewing.

Alphonse Mattia tries to imagine how a piece will look, then does a series of freehand sketches to give a general idea of the finished piece. He spends very little time on exact drawings.

On the other hand, David Ebner makes full-sized drawings, which help him to better visualize the proportions of a new piece.

When the planning stage is complete, the serious work with wood begins. Here, too, each furniture-maker has his or her own style of working. One person may rely on machines to prepare large pieces to the point where hand tools can be used. Another may engineer a piece by machine almost to its finished state. A few just do design and leave all the woodworking to expert carpenters. Today, fine craftsmanship no longer means only handmade.

Some furniture-makers prefer working alone in their shops. Others may employ an apprentice, or student, learning the craft. Still others may employ skilled assistants. The furniture-maker's needs determine whether one, two, or ten workers are hired.

Rosanne Somerson loves working with her hands. Yet she finds some tasks repetitive and boring. "On days when there's lots of sanding to do, I dread going down to the shop," she acknowledges. "Also, it's no fun making eight little drawers exactly alike." That's when Somerson calls in her assistant.

David Ebner's assistant does most of the machine cuttings and basic joinery. "He's better at it than I am," Ebner says, "because he spends more time at it."

Ebner selects the wood and does any intricate joinery and rough carving. His main role, he explains, is to find answers to problems in the design and construction of pieces. "Engineering chairs can be difficult. I want a chair to be comfortable, strong, and airy."

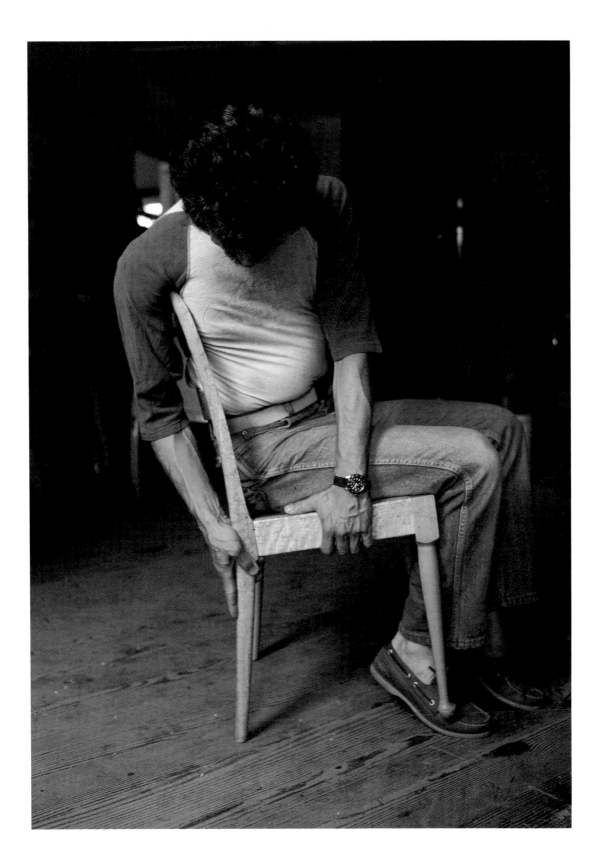

A woodworker's greatest challenge, explains Ebner, is understanding the nature of the wood and learning to work within its limits. Wood expands in damp weather and contracts in cold. A piece made in the warm climate of southern California will react differently to the fluctuating climate of New York City. Furniture design must make allowances for the response of wood to its environment. Otherwise, drawers will remain stuck shut and tabletops will split.

OAK: Strong, long-lasting, beautiful grain.

ZEBRA: Unusual grain. Skill is necessary to avoid a garish effect.

CHERRY: Smooth grain, lustrous color.

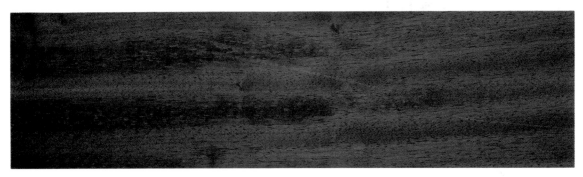

PADAUK: Rich color, hard, strong, solid.

Cocobolo: Exotic, hard, durable.

Maple: Firm, smooth, fairly heavy and strong. Not durable outdoors.

Walnut: Strong, stable, easy to carve.

Pearwood: Rich color, stable, easy to carve.

Wood is not only a temperamental medium for an artist to work in, it is also expensive. Furniture-makers have other expenses as well: rent, utilities, and general upkeep for their shops; salaries to assistants, bookkeepers, and accountants; packing and shipping costs involved in filling orders. Promotional brochures and exhibiting work at crafts centers and fairs, in hope of making sales, also cost money. To cover these expenses and make a living too, furniture-makers try to work faster and produce more.

When Graham Blackburn gets an order for twelve dining-room chairs, he designs and constructs the first and his apprentice makes the other eleven. "I make sure he keeps the measurements exact and personally teach him the carving. Then I get busy on the next project," says Blackburn.

Blackburn confesses that he relies on hand power tools more and more to save time. However, he still uses his antique hand tools when carving, making final fittings, and finishing. "There's no tool made today that has a fine an edge as an old one," he says. "Besides, I love knowing a craftsman of long ago held the tool I'm working with."

Each morning, Graham Blackburn spends the first twenty minutes of his workday sharpening the edges of his hand tools. Removable irons from planes, irons from chisels, scraper blades, and spokeshaves each get rubbed across a whetstone that has been soaking a few minutes. When Blackburn feels the edges are "sharp enough to shave the hair off your arm," he adds two or three drops of oil to the blades to prevent rust.

Some woodworkers prefer to sharpen their tools with machines that have grinding and polishing wheels, because the machines are quicker.

Regardless of which process they prefer, all furniture-makers agree that they work best when their tools are organized and in good condition. "If you know where a tool is," says Blackburn, "you don't have to think. You just reach out and there it is."

TENON SAWS: Cutting through wood

BIT BRACE: Drilling holes in wood

PANEL PLANE and STANLEY JACK PLANE: Smoothing straight surfaces

CIRCULAR WOODEN PLANE and MODERN METAL CIRCULAR PLANE: Smoothing curved surfaces

The design and function of antique and modern cabinetmaker's hand tools do not differ much.

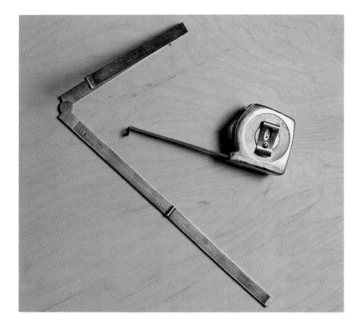

FOUR-FOLD TWO-FOOT RULE and TAPE MEASURE: Measuring

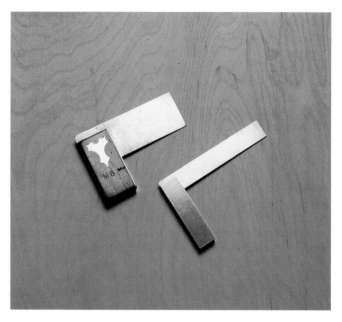

SQUARE: Marking a line at right angles to the edge

CHISEL and CONTEMPORARY JAPANESE CHISEL: Trimming wood, clearing waste from joints, and paring

CUTTING GAUGE and MARKING GAUGE: Marking a line parallel to the edge of a piece of lumber

The antique tools shown with their modern counterparts are more than two hundred years old.

Alphonse Mattia and Rosanne Somerson use power tools for almost all wood preparation and flat surface cuttings. However, they handcraft the assembly and finishing of their furniture in the manner of craftsmen of long ago. "It may be a slower process than machine work, but it gives me more artistic control," Mattia explains. "Besides, machines dictate what you can and cannot do. When you handcraft, you're in charge."

Somerson and Mattia also believe that many of the old techniques of assembly, which have made antiques last, make sense today. "There's no better fitting than a dovetail," says Somerson. She does, however, sometimes incorporate new materials, such as nylon or aluminum or a hidden touch-lock, if doing so enhances the piece. "I think of my furniture as my children," she declares. "I want them to have the best of the old and new, and I want them to be as wonderful as I can make them."

David Ebner uses machines to a far greater extent than Blackburn, Somerson, or Mattia, but he likes to hand-carve the bent parts and does all his own finishing.

Whether furniture-makers work with hand tools or powered ones, they all strive to create one-of-a-kind, finely crafted pieces. They work hard, but they enjoy what they do. As Rosanne Somerson says, "My job and my hobby are the same. I look at the world as both work and pleasure."

The author and the photographer wish to thank the artists
for their time and their cooperation:

Graham Blackburn
P.O. Box 487
Bearsville, New York 12409
and
2840 South Rodeo Gulch Road
Soquel, California 95073

David Ebner
12 Bell Street
Bellport, New York 11713

Alphonse Mattia
Rosanne Somerson
771 Division Road
Westport, Massachusetts 02790

Special thanks to the Museum of Transportation in Brookline, Massachusetts,
for allowing us to use their facilities.

Maxine B. Rosenberg was born and grew up in New York City, where she received a Bachelor of Arts degree in history and a Master of Science degree in special education from Hunter College. As a teacher and now as a full-time writer, she has honed her ability to discover the inner feelings, hopes, and ideas of others, including the artists she got to know for this book. The author of five other children's books with photographs by George Ancona, including ALA Notable Books *My Friend Leslie* and *Being Adopted*, she lives with her family in Briarcliff, New York.

George Ancona brings his own special artistry to the challenge of photographing an aesthetic subject. His award-winning photographs, known for their freshness and honesty, have appeared in over three dozen children's books, many of which he has written himself. He has worked as a designer, art director, film-maker, and professional photographer, and now handles free-lance projects from his own studio. A native of New York City, Mr. Ancona lives in Stony Point, New York.